# NOTES TO THE READER

Notes to the Reader: From Forgotten Books
Recent Work Press
Canberra, Australia

Copyright © Shane Strange 2015

All rights reserved. This book is copyright. Except for private study, research, criticism or reviews as permitted under the Copyright Act, no part of this book may be reproduced stored in a retrieval system, or transmitted in any form by any means without prior written permission. Enquiries should be addressed to the publisher.

ISBN: 978-0-9944565-8-8

# NOTES TO THE READER

*from Forgotten Books*

Shane Strange

RECENT
WORK
PRESS

# INTRODUCTION

*'This book is like any other book. But I would be happy if it were read by people whose soul was already formed.' – Clarice Lispector*

The above prescription, taken from the front matter of Clarice Lispector's *The Passion According to G.H.*, had a profound and surprising effect on me. It seemed an audacious request on the author's part. Was it possible that the audience for the book might be circumscribed by such a request? Did it mark a kind of conceit on behalf of the author? (Was my soul, as a reader, already formed?) Or did it mark a genuinely felt plea for the requisite qualities necessary to tackle the book? I was both delighted and intrigued by the idea that an author might make such a request, and in such bold and unwavering terms. I was, in fact, arrested by it and could read no further. So began what for me has been many years of collecting these exhortations, these odd paratexts, these authorial instructions (a selection of which I present here).

Recently, I have been approached by the representative of an obscure group of archivists who wish to digitise my collection, and make it available to a wider public. (How they heard of the collection, I do not know. This has been a strictly private pursuit!) I have resisted to this point. Not, it must be noted, out of some reverence to printed matter, or an unspecified fear of progress. My interest in these brief passages grew quickly to the point that I was no longer interested in the books to which they were appended. These brief authorial commands became like poetry; the books that followed: lengthy and unnecessary appendices. As a result, I stopped recording the volumes from which they came. They seemed unimportant. And so I confess to the lack of vigilance required on my part for the collection to be usefully employed in serious circles. Hence, my resistance to their broader dissemination.

    In other circles, I understand there are whispers of scepticism in relation to the collection. The charge being that I did not record the volumes from where these passages were taken, as these volumes do not exist. The collection, so goes the charge, is a conceit of my own invention. It is not the purpose of this brief introduction to deny such things, I leave judgement on these questions to the reader. All I can do is vouch for my honesty: a judgement the perspicacious reader will no doubt arrive at independently.

This book is like any other book. You may have found it in a bookstore, or borrowed it from a library. Perhaps you have purchased it in a charity sale, or inherited it from a dead uncle. Perhaps you have stolen this book, maybe from necessity; maybe from adventure. Whatever the mean of acquisition, whether money has been exchanged or not, I beg of you not to read it. Let me be clear. Do not read this book under any circumstance!

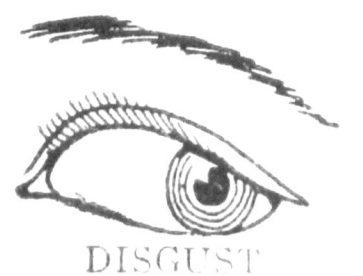

DISGUST

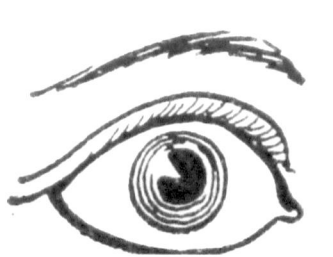

This book is to be worn in public, possibly against a particular colour of shirt, or in concert with some form of scarf or necktie. If asked, the reader should comment on 'The Writing' in as breathless a way as possible, as if describing an epiphany, or the birth of a child. If one tires of the book, a newer one will be available in the spring.

This book is a book of anticipation. You will soon note that, beyond this brief preface it has no words. Instead, dear reader, you must divine what happens. We do not recommend looking for clues in the fabric of the book. There are none. We do recommend writing down any thoughts or passages as they come to you in the blank pages of the book. These will be needed as guideposts as the story becomes more complex. Do not rely on your memory. It has failed even those with eidetic powers of recall. After some time you will mark two characters as strangely familiar. One is your father as a young man. The other is you upon finishing the book.

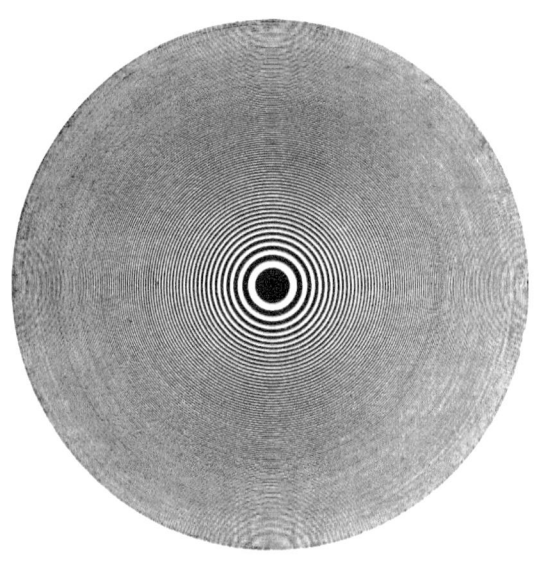

This book has no corporeal substance, but is referenced in many books of holy orders and new age philosophies, in psychoanalysis and quantum mechanics. However there is little concrete knowledge of the book. Scientists have taken to employing highly specific and sensitive machinery in the hope of measuring its effects, but to date no data of any significance can be reported. Literary analysis fares no better. The engagement of super computers to examine large volumes of text reveals only complex patterns of dots and semicircular glyphs that are suspected to refer to variations in colour on the ultraviolet scale. The full text will, of course, be revealed at the moment of death, but it will be by then too late to add to the store of human knowledge.

This book is a celebration of me. I know that for some years now, I have been coasting on material created by others. But my genius has been not to hide or obfuscate this fact, but to construct an elaborate schema that not only permits me to get away with this, but has become the source of my fame and renown. I am a purveyor of my own deceit in respectable circles, yet for this I am offered— no begged—to speak in lecture theatres, to offer opinions on irrelevant topics, to extract lessons from my work for commercial purposes, and to publish—a result of which you hold in your hand.

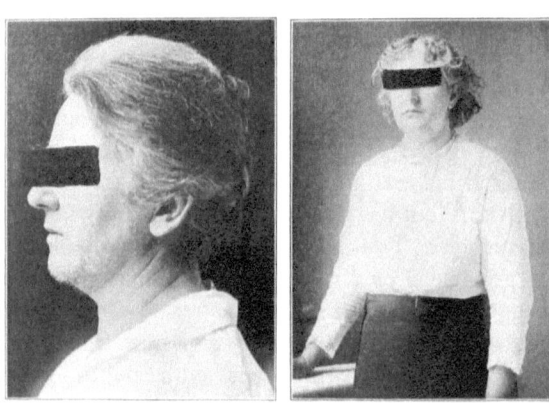

This book is a compilation of archival material found abandoned in the attic of an old museum in a metropolitan centre. I would like to say that I have filtered the material through a modern sensibility but, truth be told, I have done nothing. You read this as I have found it. Prepare yourself.

Fig. 29. Fig. 30.

This book is a contract. The reader (known hereafter as 'the reader') promises the author (known hereafter as 'the author') that they will read the text herein (known hereafter as 'the text'). The reader and the author both promise to construct each other ideally, and to varying degrees of perfection (known hereafter as, in the case of the author, 'the perfect reader' and, in the case of the reader as 'the imagined author'). Falling short of this ideal, both parties promise to displace any disappointment into literary discussions, or general fandom, in the case of the reader; and manifestos of divine inspiration/imagination/craft, in the case of the author. Any form of prosopopeiac act performed by the author is an illusion. This contract is not binding on either party and, subject to acts of God, should be broken at will.

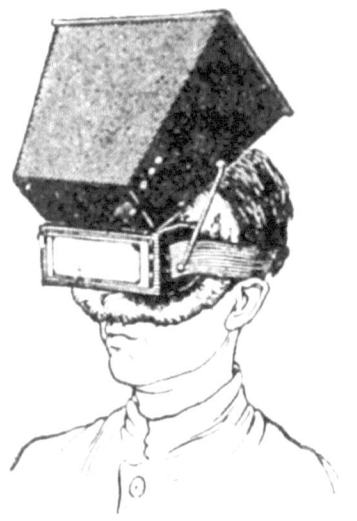

This book is the book of selfishness. With each page, even the most outward facing and empathic reader will begin to find thoughts of themselves dominating interactions with intimate friends. You will want to claim things, to put your name on them. You will accept and seek systems of informal patronage. You will dismiss people outright for their lack of utility. You will develop the capacity to reduce a situation to a bare calculus of self advancement. You will pronounce on your autonomy, though you will demand the assistance of, and be supported by, many. There will never be enough money to 'make a living'. You will hedge and justify. You will develop envy into a fine art form. Nothing will be good enough. You will always claim you are undervalued.

This book can only be comprehended by animals. Its meanings vary according to the level of domesticity. Cats, dogs, goldfish, budgerigars, guinea pigs etc. are convinced the book is about suburban decay. Wilder animals (kangaroos; tigers; larger species of moth; monitor lizards) maintain it revolves around the protagonist's struggle to transform against overwhelming odds. Some smaller forms of bird life and most major reptile families ask that we look to the minor characters to understand the text, while more obscure arthropods suggest that we look to what the text does not say. Newer discoveries are being made daily by as yet unnamed sea creatures in the depths of the Indian Ocean, though their reading practices are thought to rely too heavily on the Russian formalist school. Animals bred to be eaten (cows, chickens, pigs etc.) are merely grateful for the distraction.

This book can only be read in queues, preferably in Japan, where there are rules of politeness in relation to waiting. For the daring, however, any anglophone country will suffice, particularly those that admire the formation of queues in the abstract when applied to issues of inhumanity, but disregards them practically when applied to issues of wealth and privilege. The reader should be warned that in some instances the book will need to be read behind razor wire. For their own safety, the book should not be read by small children.

This book is like any other book. But it should be read by those with romantic notions of the past. The cities you find in this book will never be as you imagined them, the technology never as quaint. There will be smells you cannot account for, and differing standards of personal hygiene. Do not look for good dental work, or height. Do expect to encounter the same general uncertainty that, in your time, marks your own life—though in some circumstances that will manifest as uncertainty about the future, and in others, uncertainty about the present's capacity to measure up to the past. Prepare to go for long periods with little food. Conceal a knife on your person, in case of unexpected civil war, or the need for sudden, violent egress.

This book should not be believed under any circumstances. The author makes several claims that have no evidence base and therefore should be disregarded.

This book must be read in darkness. The text, the illustrations, the marginalia are exposed in the complete *absence* of light. The ambient light from digital alarm clocks, street lamps through window panes, or even the moon still allow the book to keep its secrets,. For the best possible chance of reading, we recommend sitting in a cupboard, wardrobe or any other enclosed space. Tape shut any gaps around and between doorways and the like. A wide gaffer tape should suffice. Some people have suggested removing to remote areas to read the book, away from urban light pollution. Experiments have been inconclusive as no one sent to test this hypothesis has ever returned.

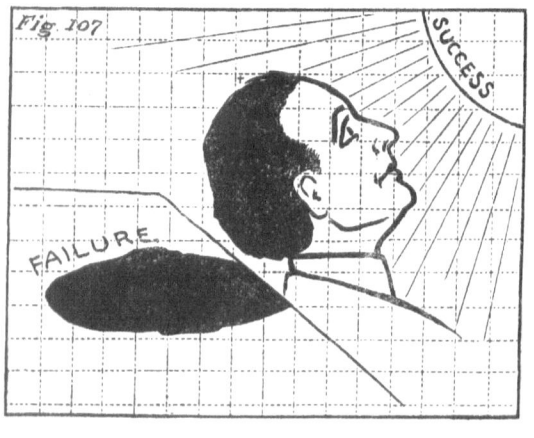

This book is a list of instructions and exhortations. Become fitter. Lead a more fulfilling life. Earn more money. Be loved. Be more spiritual. To be more productive, you must set and achieve goals. To achieve dreams, you must accept defeat. To compromise, you must comply. To be happier, you must look at the *longue durée*. You must ameliorate promises. Take the letter of the law if not the spirit. Divide your time into smaller and smaller parts. Sell it off. See things in abstraction. Be a team player. Stay positive. It will end soon. It will all end soon.

This book was written in the minutes after waking, and before preparing breakfasts and school lunches for children. As such any seemingly unfinished sentences, rushed passages, clichéd characters or fragmentary plotlines may be taken as evidence that the author exists outside the text. Stains from various foods may be found on some pages.

This book will bring forth memories of childhood. The reader should be prepared as these will be neither the saddest or happiest moments, but the most mundane: waiting for dinner to be served; waiting for parents to return from work; waiting for the school day to end; waiting to leave the supermarket; waiting for the sun to come out; waiting to be grown. It will become clear that childhood was composed of interminable periods of boredom and frustration. This realisation will force the reader to reexamine the purpose of their lives. Someone will call to say a relative has died.

THE BOGEY-OWL.

This book is the book of expectation. As a child you are taken to a party at friends of your parents. But something feels altogether different there. There is the polite tinkling of laughter, studied kindnesses offered and returned. There is conversation, not gossip. There are sparkling glasses and rooms furnished with what you later come to identify as taste. In the thick magazines placed on a table you see an advertisement where men in tailored suits drink tumblers of liquor around a billiard table, while beautifully dressed woman watch from the bar across the room. The advertisement says 'For those who have arrived.' You vow that your life will be that life—one of arrival— and you begin to plot your escape. From that point on you convince yourself that each miserable day is the prelude to something better. You tell yourself that all that surrounds you, all the yelling and bad behaviour, is ephemeral, that all pleasures should be deferred, while all miseries suffered in the moment. As you grow the experience of each of your hopes disappoints you in turn, until they are exhausted. You are exhausted. The moment has never arrived. You have never arrived.

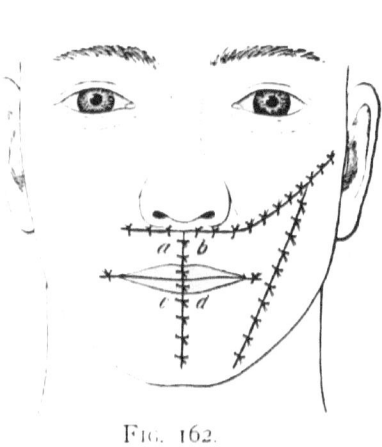

Fig. 162.

This book is the book of revolutions. At a party at a friend's house, you will meet someone who will incoherently mention the movement in question. Not knowing if you have heard them correctly, you will try to confirm what you have heard only to find the person has disappeared. Later, in an alley off a dark square, you will be let into a small bar previously unknown to you, where a group of bearded men will be discussing the revolution in undertones. You will watch them until you are asked to leave by the bartender, who thinks you are an informer. After some time, you will be asked to help distribute a newspaper, the organ of the movement. And later again, you will fight enemies in running street battles outside automobile factories. You will be cut across the face with a broken bottle, scarring your cheek. Still later, there will be internal ructions and irrevocable splits in the movement. Though your differences are small, you will have no other choice than to join a splinter group. Dwindling resources and flagging spirits will cause the closure of the group's newspaper, and with your comrades you will take to drinking in a previously unknown bar, discussing strategy and theory well into the night. One day, you will run into an old friend on the street. He will tell you that you look unwell. You confess that things have not been good for you in recent times and that you are questioning your involvement in the movement. He invites you to a party at his house later that week where, forgetting how to act in polite company, you will drink too much and pass out under a table. In the morning you will be told that you were making unguarded remarks about the movement. Your friend counsels that this may have been unwise. He could not be sure of anyone who might have been listening.

This book is a book for travellers. In anxious moments in unfamiliar cities, it will remind you of home: in each paragraph, a street from your home town; in each sentence a friend. Sit and read it with coffee, or strange wine, or the milk from a surprising animal, or a dark red pilsener. Do not store too much pleasure in it. The purpose of travel is to be slightly uneasy, slightly afraid. This is the basis of surprise and delight. The book is not to be held in front of you like a shield, or referred to in conversation. If you meet someone who claims to have read the book, make an excuse and hurry away. In time they will eat you, and carry your carcass back home like a trophy.

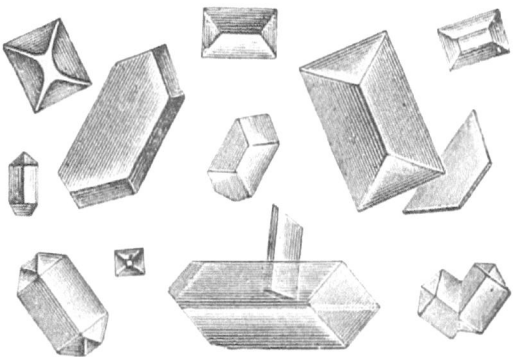

This book will remain unread. Although you have the most earnest intentions to turn the page and begin, something, perhaps a distraction or memory, or perhaps feeling of discomfort or incompleteness will overtake you. You will put the book down and not pick it up again. When asked you will claim it was brilliant.

# More Recent Work

| | |
|---:|:---|
| Owen Bullock | *Urban Haiku (2015)* |
| | *River's Edge (2016)* |
| Paul Hetherington | *Gallery of Antique Art (2016)* |
| Prose Poetry Project | *Pulse (2016)* |
| Subhash Jaireth | *Incantations (2016)* |
| Niloofar Fanaiyan | *Transit (2016)* |
| Jen Webb | *Sentences from the Archive (2016)* |
| Monica Carroll, Jen Crawford, Owen Bullock & Shane Strange | *5,6,7,8 (2016)* |
| Shane Strange | *Notes to the Reader (2015)* |

all titles available from
recentworkpress.com